I Messaged My Ex

We shared, then I missed her
On a journey, now just mine
Till maybe I can love again?

Samuel L. Field

www.samuelfield.com

Cataloguing-in-Publication entry is available
from the National Library of Australia
http://catalogue.nla.gov.au

First published 2022 by YndFwd

www.yndfwd.com/Publishing

Contents

Is there a treaty
we could sign?

I don't know what truce would work
I've mulled it over since we split

The Chasm

As I saw your shadow
Crossing pains wide chasm
I tried to stop my reaching
To keep my hope in check

As I leaned out of safety
I feared my own intent
Yet fears fell from sight
As I saw your hair fall

Hair cascading down neck
Bouncing softly over breasts
My fears fell lightly weighted
From my eyes, yet not to rest

Leaving you and me
With little between us
But the clothes of shame
Maybe the scent of regret

Love had burned a pilot light
Three years and then some
Now its out of its shield
I must face why it hid

Bondage of self
By fear and inaction
Or freely following me
Bifurcation called choice

My flame to pursue
Living not nursing
Pain be damned
Or it dams me

Will you burn for me?
Can we dis-arm hearts?
Stepping over pain together
Shall we dance?

Could we love again?

I had love
I had a lot to give

I was scared to let go
I wanted some control

You had hurt me
Maybe you had love

Maybe you had stuff to give
Maybe you were scared too

If you could try
...I would too!

Our Magic?

When did unmet need
Become all the magic between us?

Hope is a powerful fuel
Why do I burn it to get no progress?

Crossing over

When I saw you
On this new side of intimacy
More distance between our souls

We all change
I loved who I knew
But is that you still?

My ex's kiss

Why did you kiss me?
Why ask that now
You had left clearly
You had said it loud

I had been moving away
I am moving along
I was accepting
Your closure of our song

You kissed me quickly
It wasn't very long
It wasn't committed
No new verse in view

The kiss was a question
You want me to want
To keep that door open
For your use, not mine

You want me to be
A safe connection for you
But that's not reciprocal
Its not been for years

It is not right to kiss me
Don't knock on my door
Asking that question
Then run into night

What you didn't say

Started to hear it on your lips
Then you sided it to pits
Keeping back that car

Maybe words of desire
Or ones of healing
Maybe a sorry

Yet you sidelined
Potential connection
Off tracks I kept clear

Invisible me

Invisibility unbecomes me
Yet its curse holds me fast
She can't see or hear me
But with all my world I yell

Hear me, see me
I offer you myself
I ask so little in return
Alone, I still yearn

Is this done?

I have yearned so much for closeness
I am sure it had scared you
Closeness has rarely been safe for you
I don't think you're perfect
In fact, I know you're not

My love for you is not just desire
But of that, there is a lot
Yet I can't love you as I do
It hurts too much
I can't stand so close
I keep wanting to touch

So I'll back away
Not cause I'm done
But because I'm not

Pulling back

Something come to mind
I was thinking you over
Even last night

Miss your hugs and your smile
Your presence there by my side
Your jokes and turns of humor
Our slow build of shared musings

I almost text-ed to say
That I was missing you in that way
But, then I fly far away
And send just a pic the next day

How do I move on, while
loving you?

Will it split me
Or make me
More ...

Your mark

Long before
Your name
Was tattooed on my arm
It was etched across my heart

While you no longer
Touch my toes when we sleep
Hold my arm when we walk
This etching may always remain

Am I still where we connected

The memory of your presence
Sharing life with you
Anchors me to you
Drives my heart to
Want plowed the road
Between where you are now
And where I am still

Unique Love

I loved you in ways
I may never love another
I loved with my soul
With all my care
With my heart sleeves
Dangling just there

I loved you like it would never end
Like you could never hurt another
Your beautiful soul was desired
You were my best friend
I loved you in ways
I may never again
Love another

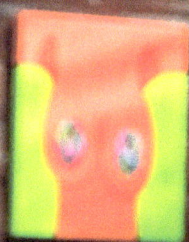

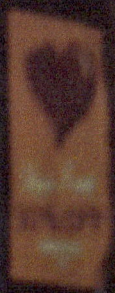

Wrong Farming

So long I believed in the fertile soil of us
It felt so rich when we first planted
Then several seasons in
Our crops failed
We had fertilised
With the wrong shit

You are a drug

My head is rumbling
My veins are on fire
My heart is wired
I haven't done drugs
I'm strung out on desire

Your looks are my poison
Your words are live wires
Your eyes melt manhood
I listen for a humming
Your buzz of desire

Yet your expressions, empty
I want your love
Craving your feelings, mutual desire
This withdrawal...
oh Hope I am strung out on desire

Away

My scrambled egg brain
Just wanting to avoid pain
When my heart wanted
To run, yet to stay

I wanted it to rain
I never learn't those steps
So storms came along
But not the rain I craved

I chased your attention
Your favour, your rain
Yet you moved on
...away

Missed your connection

You had drifted, yet
The boat of our love
Anchored to my heart
And this anchor held fast

You might have re-cast
But it cannot re-grounded
You can't anchor elsewhere
It's still bound to my heart

I want to be free
Yet I want you back
I miss the tug on my heart
When you're pulling my chain

Your humor is rough
Your skin is so not
Your love's truth
Is hidden well

Let your light shine
Let it shine for me
Or let it not

Come or go
But let it be known
I wanted you to stay

Ghost of Her

My wife ghost keeps visiting me
She comes to mind when I'm alone
We talk, mostly about what was
Left unresolved between us
When my wife, shes was

There's no point to these visits
They are all about the past
She isn't doing any of the resolving
So I started saying no
She visits too much

Sometimes it's worse
When she who was calls
And we speak on the phone
She and I don't talk direct and clear
I've tried and she doesn't hear me

I don't know what she hears
Some echo on the line
Maybe of words past
Time to stop practicing
With my wife's ghost

I am Shot

Feeling shot
I'm drinking a lot
Every time
You enter my head
I feel a little life
A-lot of dread
Before that passes
I'll reach for the glass
Another shot to the head

I'm waking a lot
Not refreshed but drained
Keep debating how
I'm staying sane
Why do I want you?
You hurt me so
It's love
Baby that's how I know

Trying to rest
I'm feeling beat
Closed my eyes
Yet I can't just sleep
This escapes me
Like her love has too
Leaving me waiting
Under this half moon

Only Move

Been walking since 6 am
Just stopped to rest a bit
Travel plans not cleared
But I guess that's fine
Can't find peace of mind
The watch says 14+ clicks
That's a solid distance it is
I'm not sure what I'll do

Walked past the jetty twice
The reminder of you
Of love and loss
Hopes not renewed
I walked around it
I walked past
It was too hard
Remembering you

I want you still
I want you now
I don't understand it
Probably never will
I just wanted it mutual
It was once I felt
Thought I sensed it in you
Maybe I sensed it in myself

I hope you are happy
I can't bear to ask
I wanted to be happy
With you
But that didn't last
I can't rebuild alone
Today, I can only move

Cut you out of my life!

Should I cut you from my life
Lowering you from my mind
Each time you start to enter
Brain bouncers ejecting you

Could I cut you from my memory
Edit out your references
Cutting out your pictures
Leaving a void relief of your shadow

Would I cut my heart so small
If I dice you from there
I'd cut so much
I'd cut me too

I loved you with
a Love...

Leaving it behind me
Not in front of me

Heart Slippers

We talk but don't connect
She cannot see me it seems
I say some words with intent
Failing to reach the mark
The woman I deeply loved
Then it was construed
Into her construction
False image already
Acting as a stand in
For me, for her

Measured words stutter
Feeling pathetic
Mixed in desire to connect
I dodge the broken glass
Surrounding her soul's depth
As long as I have known her
I try to walk the approach
Wearing heart skinned slippers

My damage
Heart tissue scars
Approach is painful
For her it must be
Isolating too
Her memories of pain
Clouding views of others
All who tried
Eventually leave
How can I show love?
The lens was never clear
Her heart waiting for hurt
Eventually I did too

Smoke it out

I wanted to write my heart out
In a cloud of smoking ruins
To pour my anger into
Well worn grooves
Yet my heart is not a slave
Or even so simple

I want to be angry
Because I am still hurting
I want to be angry
To burn away the pain
I want to be angry
To numb the loneliness of now

I want to be angry
Because I am still believing
In love and partnership
And having that again
it's just...
Not Now

Dusty Romance

What is romance but dust?
Blowing in the wind, then gone
Colouring air as it drifts down slowly
I watch the setting sun and contemplate
It has a golden arc ablaze in falling beauty
The sun pours through it, to warm my heart
As I am beholding this sight and frozen
An unexpected moment of softness
Because my heart is still beating
Blood is warm in this body
My body made of dust

Un-Love

I can't un-love you
Too much of me
Loved too much of you
To cut it from my heart

I can only hope
To love another more
To make a blinding light
Of a love even deeper
A new star birth

Not that loss won't hurt any longer
Or that part of me won't care as much
But these new heart's extensions of mine
Will care, will love even more in new ways

To our therapist

Long time since I've been in for a session
Been um'ng about coming in it feels forever
I debated which therapist to see
I felt returning to you
Would be to be
With her you see
Yet I didn't want to go elsewhere
I wasn't fully ready
To let go
To admit defeat
To surrender my love
Somehow incomplete

I stopped writing mostly
I just edited the old
I collected into books
One has been sold
She calls it a book of hate
Though she hasn't read any pages
She holds my emotions at bay
Yet I have kept waiting

Eventually, I wrote again
At first just to be in a flow
I died little deaths
It had taken me slowly
Pausing my life

My connections
Afraid of my real intentions
I loved her deep somewhere
But I didn't like that I do
I started to write
Then couldn't lie to me

I couldn't hold it in
I haven't shown her
She doesn't want me
She has told me

I felt like me
I feel so lost
Trying to piece together
My own fragments
Trying to see
Now who I can be

Sunken Jetty

Passing the sunken jetty
Sitting in the river calmly
It's bleached white posts
Joining lunar reflections

Its day has ended
As night has come
Now sinking slowly
Peaceful surrender

Beautiful brokenness
Surrender to bring peace
Future storms unsurvivable
Yet tonight it sleeps

A watery omen seen
What our loves
Have come to be
Slow surrender

Our broken beauty
Yet in calm can see
What was once
Strong, complete

Its day has past
I mourn it no more
Its job now complete
There is beauty in sleep

See you later

I never said good bye
Maybe I never wanted it to end
I definitely wanted to run
But really wanted to have
My best friend back
I over looked your flaws
Your lack of clear intent
You had been surviving
It wasn't connecting
I wanted connect

A Love

I love you with a love
That doesn't know how to quit
It holds its breath when you take
Your time to reply
Our wit is so quick
Our banter is usually shallow
Expressions of love
Heartfelt hugs
They don't come thick

I love you with a love
That has held me hostage
It's threatened to overwhelm me
Its hold is caustic
It hasn't set me free
It won't let me be
It calls and pushes me
Bound my hands
Legs are free
But I can't run you see

I love you with a love
That has seared my heart alive
It was aware through the pain
Yet it still burns with desire
Your beauty captivates me
Though my heart is forlorn
The drink I want to drown
Is the taste of your love
But that cork is holding on

I love you with a love
From which no good can come
You're still learning to love yourself
You have been going that way so long
You don't love me back
I got that wrong
Yet I know it so deeply
I love you with a love
That must be strong

I love you with a love
That wanted to see your underneath
To touch your perfect flaws
To embrace your incomplete
To be each other's glue
Cheerleaders each
On our journeys complete
That's not what you wanted
In love we didn't meet

I love you with a love
From hair to your feet
I saw your hidden shadow
Your aging physique
I yearned intimately
But you wanted different
You wanted shallow
And I wanted deep

I loved you with a love
That offered all I had
I provided more than that
I wanted to be glad
To change in any way
To suit your taste in men
Twisting me was lame
In the end, I learned
I was only your friend

I loved you with a love
That offered you my heart
In the end, you broke it
I still didn't walk far
How I tried to mend myself
And reach your brokenness
I nearly lost my way
Across your distantness

I loved you with a love
That accepted your token-ness
Yet it broke each time I hoped
For openness
Yet I yearned for your tokens
My offering was a full return
I hoped you would
See the difference
And open up your world

I had loved with a love.
Now it's time has come
The love is holding me bound
It's holding me strong
It has no road back
It's been sinking too long
It's going to be no fun
Untangling the ropes
Of my love that are so long

What Kind of Ghost?

Laying in bed
Nearly asleep
Whats that noise?
What kind of ghost?
Sounding like you
Yet just the echo of memories
Reverb'ing in the stillness of my now

Never Like This

I loved you in many ways
I may never love another
I loved with my soul
With my deepest care

With my heart sleeves
Freely dangling against you
Like we could never
Hurt each other

I loved you like it
Could never end
I loved you in ways
I may never love another

Bland Status Change

Not being one to just change a status
Waiting to see it on faces
Their surprise
Or otherwise

Life takes us down roads
So many we don't plan
We don't choose to go on

We don't want or plant crops to stay in
We have to just accept what is and move on
Deal with what is, make good decisions

Shaved my head, something major has ended
Smoked a cigar and drank whisky
With a very good friend

On this post
I didn't want to just change my status
Blandly to divorced

Can I love again?

Can I?

Avoiding connection

I loved, I didn't protect me
I loved, I over looked
I loved, I let you in
I loved, so deep
You were in so deep
I thought you would never leave

Maybe I will never love again
Can I take back what I gave
My love was yours to keep
But you threw that away
I'm picking up my pieces
Building a new shaped me

Maybe I can love again
Could I step over the line?
Committing heart deeply
There is beauty in deep love
Can I find someone special
To build deep beauty with me?

She Was Right

You were right
I am scared
Scared to move left
Or even right
To open again
My heart to new light
If I let someone in
What would I loose
I worked so hard
Getting out of a noose
If I don't I'll be alone
I know that pain well
So in reverse could I go?
Would the tree grow again
How could I know
I Was safe
From an Axe
I could not have known

My Deepest Fear

We crowd around the bar
Strangers each leaning in a way
A night part way and sharing is too
Seeking comfort as we stumble stories
Finding ways to know another

Three drinks I was asked clear
"What was my deepest fear?"
I looked the asker in the eyes
Deciding to be vulnerable
I put weight on my answer
Letting someone in

I write poetry
Sharing deep exploration
I have left open so many doors
Leaving all with angled views
I have moved on from those spaces
I'm deeper than places I let you see

Now struggling to trust again
How to let someone new
In a room I am still alive in
Sharing this life I'm in today
Where you can touch me
Where I can still be hurt

Showing rooms I have left is safe
Some are already damaged
Sure that was painful
But I don't live there
I just cracked a door
On way down to deeper levels
How do I open the door on my heart today?

Longing

Where do I bear my soul?
To whom shall I be unashamedly true
My weaknesses, my faults
My deepest recesses

She asks for my strengths
When confidence glows
My handsome repose
My manly restraint

Where is my safety?
Where do I collapse
In what lovers arms
With not just my body naked

I want to be before another
My strengths and weakness
Naked and embraced as me
As I am, all ways, complete

Real love is

Kind
Gentle
Wants no harm
Keeps no record of wrong

Love is

Love is not a victory march,
Nor is it a death stare.
It's a chosen connection,
To love another through,
One imperfection at a time.

Perfection needs not love.
Our flaws, our canvas,
That we paint love onto.
One choice at a time,
Love gifted, unearned.

A perfect canvas is smooth,
As love is easily applied upon,
Yet mine is cracked and imperfect.
To these cracks more love was given.

I too will be a painter.
Bring your broken canvas,
Rejected by other painters,
I will cover it in deep love.

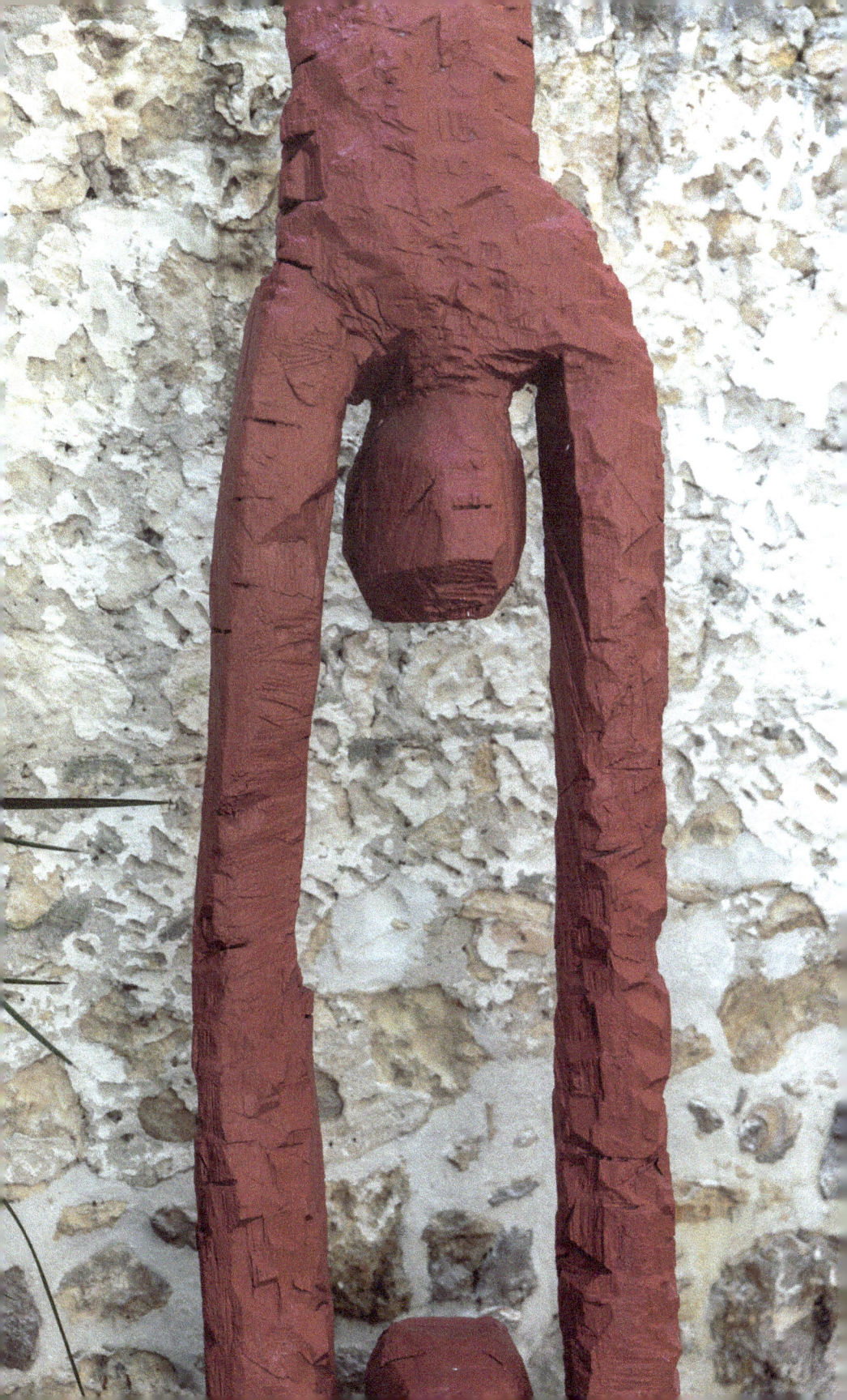

Time and Tide

It was a cool morning
To watch the day settle
Into action from a beach
Coffee and a slow walk
On each leg I saw the man
Bent on the beach
He wrote in the sand
Of his love and loss
Her beauty, her grace
Of his care for her
Listing his names
Names for love
There are deeply held
And must be for so long
To be repeated in sand
Persistent love memories
Rewritten in shifting times
Every way, every wave
Every week
Drawing over again
From his timeless drink
To bring in someway
What was into this now
But what has past
Carried on a different wave
She has been taken from him

Like his words and waves
But neither has taken away
His deep heart

Sharing a Beat

This beat I am hearing
A rhythm from my life
I dance the beat of
It calls me along
High and down
In and deeper

I thought you would hear it too
I thought we could share
I thought I could dance with you
I learned to dance alone
I follow my own beat
I dance it well now

Maybe another will hear it too
I will see their music's steps too
Learning to share, dance together
Tuning into hearts channel
Taking turns, joint steps
Feel each beat through

Given in trust

I believe in a shared journey
I believe in commitment
I hold to a special union
A union with another

I anchor on mutual trust
This union true and fast
Grounding in flooding
And shelter in fire

Respect is my guarantee
Honesty is a deep key
Unity is my reward
Loves true return

I need no ceremony
I need no ring
My hearts true hold
I give in trust

Intimacy is Sharing

The magic of intimacy
Depths of its safety
Majesty of grace
Hearts entwined
Sharing deepest spaces

Love Phases

What bittersweet thing can be love
Awakening hearts and drawing you in
Then waxing and waning
Coming in waves and changes
Like seasons or lunar phases

Fast as a river
Settled as deep water
Coming differently at each approach
Sometimes we are washed away
Sometimes, leaving behind a lighter load

I have found
I have walked away
I have tasted the ocean
I have been the shoal water
Love is beautiful, kind, wants no harm
True love heals even when everything turns

Yearn

Yearning to know, but fearful
If I pull open hearts curtain
Show you the tears of my soul
Will I blind you?
If you start to know
Would you then see
Me beyond brokenness

My soul needs your mercy
But I want more than pity
See potential
I desire
We lift each up
Not from our mess
But through beauty to skies

For Sale : 1 Heart

One used heart for sale:
I've upped the purchase price
Last time I traded it for attention
This time its a fair exchange
My heart for yours

ANTIBALAS
AFROBEAT
ORCHESTRA

TIJUANA
CARTEL

LITTLE BIRDY

Katy

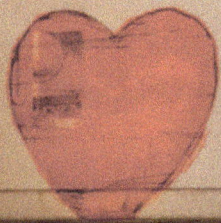

LITTLE BIRDY

GORILLAZ
DEMON DAYS

NEW ALBUM
OUT NOW

TOTALLY
HUGE

DJ

FESTIVAL

Alley Way
-Melbourne

South Bank
-Melbourne

Street Artist
-Melbourne

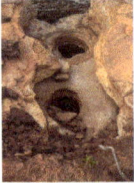

Rock Pools
-Broome

Pavement
-Indonesia

Boat
-Yarra River

Dune
-Myalup

Duyfken
-Swan River

Gantheaume Point -Broome

Atlantis
-Two Rocks

Gallery Window
-Moores Building
Fremantle

Hosier Lane
-Melbourne

Federation
Walkway
-Perth

Wati Nyirunya
(The Man Nyiru) 2016
by Rupert Jack
-WA Museum Boola Bardip

Boutique Bar
-Northbridge

Boat Jetty
-Safety Bay

On a Dune
-Myalup

Sister on Dune
-Myalup

Heli-pad
-Cairns

Moon Cafe
-North Bridge

Mundaring Weir
-Mundaring

Train Siding
-Forest Station

Old Brewery
-Perth

Facing North
- Preston Beach

Train Line
-Forest Station

London Court
-Perth

Playground
-Myalup

Swan River
-Como

Facing SA Border
-Forest Station

Dead Jetty,
Como

Mr Walkers
-South Perth

Through Trees
-Como

Model: Kira Andrews
-Johnny Ma Studios

Power Station
-Fremantle, WA

Deck
-Kings Park, WA

Hidden
-Kings Park, WA

Daughters Toys
-Doll House

Three Sheets
-Hillarys

Power Station
-Fremantle, WA

McTaggart Cove
-CY O'Connor Reserve

Courtyard statue
-Fremantle

Beach
-Myalup

Decorations
-Guilderton

Swan River
-Applecross

Ex's Backyard
-Safety Bay

Sunset
-Indonesia

Daughters Toys
-Doll House

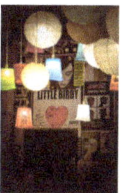
Greens & Co
-Leederville

www.ingramcontent.com/pod-product-compliance
Lightning Source LLC
Chambersburg PA
CBHW052013030426
42334CB00029BA/3203